Life is Your Soul Road

You get to cut this book up
and glue it back together.
You get to add your own
words and images.
You get to make this book
all your own, just like your
own beautiful life.

melody freebird PUBLICATIONS

cut here

Hey, Beautiful Soul!
READY TO GET STARTED?

1. Start by cutting out all of the collage sheet middle pages, (as well as these instructional pages.) You'll see the cutting line on the pages that are meant to be cut out. The images and journaling prompts found on these collage pages are designed to be cut out and pasted onto the remaining pages in your Creative Soul Searching Book. Removing the pages will also make room for the other things you may want to paste into your book. You can add all sorts of beauty!

****The best way I have found to cut out the pages is to slide a thin cutting mat under the pages and use a ruler as a cutting guide inside the cutting line while using a craft blade/knife to cut the page out. It's important to put something under the page so that you don't cut through the pages behind it. You can also use scissors if you don't have a craft blade/knife.

2. Once you have all of your collage sheet pages cut out, you are ready to begin! The possibilities are endless as you sit down to start your Creative Soul-Searching process. You can cut out journaling prompts, paste them down and then either write the thoughts, feelings and answers that come to you . . . or you can find images and words and letters from old books, junk mail, etc. to express your answers to these prompts.

3. You can add your own images from magazines, your own artwork and ESPECIALLY photos of yourself. Simply print out photos of yourself on regular copy paper with your home printer, or use a fun instant camera, or have prints of your photos made at a photo printing center. You can add stickers, stamps, light coats of craft paint or ink, patterned paper, decorative tape. I love to cut letters of the alphabet from junk mail and catalogs and write my own words in a "ransom" style . . . truly the possibilities are endless! Just have fun!

Enjoy spending this time with yourself and your beautiful soul. Make it a practice in your life - soul work is just as important as exercise and eating right. Creative Soul Searching will easily become a GOOD HABIT in your life and something you can turn to over and over again throughout your life.

Want some fun and meaningful ideas for how to use this book and the other creative soul-searching books I've made for you? Come see my soul-to-soul tutorial videos on my youtube channel called Melody Ross Media - look for the playlist called Creative Soul Searching - I will give you all sorts of fun and meaningful ideas for how to use this book with other things you have around the house or have collected. I hope to see you there, we will have so much fun together!

Don't forget to decorate your cover!

cut here

Hello Friend!

I'm Melody and I'm so happy you're here and making time for yourself and your soul. If you have never done cut & paste journaling before, get ready to get addicted! It's the most effective form of journaling that I have found for myself and my own soulwork.

So let's talk about soulwork. The world is a wearying place. We can get swept into the stress and pressure of the world so deeply that we stop hearing and knowing ourselves. When this happens, life starts to feel like a tedious chore rather than an epic adventure. And that is what life is supposed to be, even with all of it's difficulties and challenges.

Taking time to get to know ourselves as we grow and change and evolve is one of the most important investments we can make in our wellness. This book is made for exactly that.

This journal is themed around MOVING FORWARD in life, and making sure it's on YOUR OWN PATH and not the path of another. As you start to take this book apart and put it back together, keep in mind that your life is your masterpiece creation. You got to dooido what matters to you and how you will spend your minutes and your years. Enjoy creating a book about YOUR Soul Road. You are deeply loved.

melodyross

www.melodyrossmedia.com

On My
Soul Road

Life is a journey

cut here

This is
my own path.

Some journeys
you've got to
take alone.

New places
and
new faces.

It is time
for a change.

I am walking toward

I am walking away from

I am headed to

I am looking for

I am finding

I am learning about

I am healing from

I am enjoying the company of

I am really missing the company of

I am in awe of

I am letting go of

I am holding on to

I am finally seeing

I am listening to

I am becoming more

I am feeling so

life is maddening   life is exhilirating   life is wierd   life is phenomer
s an adventure life is more than what it seems   life is changing   life
life is good   life is devastating   life is chaotic   life is precious   l
is stressful   life is restorative   life is colorful   life is dull   li
s magical   life is about love   life is about learning   life is connecti
life will break you   life will grow you   life will teach you   life wil
challenge you   life will ask you   life will be relentless   life will l
ll make you what you are meant to be life will let you experience cons
going life will soften you   life will toughen you up   life will retur
fe does not give up on you   life will patiently wait for you to learn
is gorgeous life is in order life is a paradox life is a mystery l
ife is lovely life holds gifts for you life wants you to notice lif
not always fair life can transform pain into wisdom life is here to
t to be lived life is meant to be experienced life is meant to be enjo
ife will not leave you behind life is on your side life will let you l
mined life is amazing life is surprising life is difficult life is
life is educating life is transformative life is perplexing life i
ife is maddening life is exhilirating life is wierd life is phenomer
s an adventure life is more than what it seems life is changing life
ife is good life is devastating life is chaotic life is precious l
is stressful life is restorative life is colorful life is dull li
s magical life is about love life is about learning life is connecti
life will break you life will grow you life will teach you life wil
challenge you life will ask you life will be relentless life will l
ll make you what you are meant to be life will let you experience cons
going life will soften you life will toughen you up life will retur
fe does not give up on you life will patiently wait for you to learn
is gorgeous life is in order life is a paradox life is a mystery l
ife is lovely life holds gifts for you life wants you to notice lif
not always fair life can transform pain into wisdom life is here to
t to be lived life is meant to be experienced life is meant to be enjo
e will not leave you behind life is on your side life will let you le
rmined life is amazing life is surprising life is difficult life is
life is educating life is transformative life is perplexing life i
ife is maddening life is exhilirating life is wierd life is phenomer
an adventure life is more than what it seems life is changing life
ife is good life is devastating life is chaotic life is precious l
is stressful life is restorative life is colorful life is dull li
s magical life is about love life is about learning life is connecti
life will break you life will grow you life will teach you life wil
challenge you life will ask you life will be relentless life will l
l make you what you are meant to be life will let you experience cons

Life is beautiful

5 words to describe life right now:

1.

2.

3.

4.

5.

good things are going to happen

cut here

etrayed I have been betrayed I have redeemed I have fought I ha
e stayed I have been a good girl I ha been a bad girl I have mad
sorrow I have felt pea have shown the way I
nside I have been discovered I hav
e transformed I h I have breath
I have won I hav I have meant
e sung I have sp out I have
e seen I have b have g
ed I have redee been
d girl I have bee de b
e I have felt despa have
orn I have reinvente bee
ll I have fed I have-b nderst
have softly spoken se I have long
ed I have broken I ha walked away I h
t from seeds I have see them I have beer
to begin I have I have held it all
I have hated r I have seen da
I have loved I have bre my breath I
I ha otten I have en care
I have ved sile houted out hidd
d I have s shown
d I have fought I have le pea
a bad girl I have made takes

am on my own path I am recovering I am getting stronger I am phen
n good at lots of things I am okay that I am not good at everything I
am full of awe I am ready for adventure I am on a mission I am a m
I letting go I am holding on tight I am figuring it out I am often c
m a soul I am a human being I am an individual I am part of it al
am letting myself begin again I am remembering the good things I have
I am a warrior I am a gentle heart I am brave I am ready for a cha
m here to experience life I am here to love others I am here to be lo
am gutsy I am afraid of lots of things I am curious I am an artist
am a lover of music I am a lover of dancing I am a lover of people
m breathing I am thinking I am wondering I am feeling I am talkir
am reinventing I am building I am creating I am dreaming I am pla
art of creation I am looking for awe I am noticing beauty I am a na
m starting over I am celebrating I am grieving I am cleaning up a bi
am loved I am misunderstood I am seen I am heard I am not done livir
full of life I am going through hard things right now I am having a
m lucky I am blessed I am learning to accept this time in my life I a
a free spirit I am unlearning I am remembering I am revisiting I am
n in love with the earth I am a lover of color I am a happy person
nding up for what I believe in I am standing up for others I am doin
courageous I am working on my life I am focusing on self-respect I a
m powerful I am strong I am learning I am beautiful in my own wa
l I am alive I am a part of the human family I am beloved I am a m
am on my own path I am recovering I am getting stronger I am phen
n good at lots of things I am okay that I am not good at everything I
am full of awe I am ready for adventure I am on a mission I am a m
I letting go I am holding on tight I am figuring it out I am often c
m a soul I am a human being I am an individual I am part of it al
am letting myself begin again I am remembering the good things I have
I am a warrior I am a gentle heart I am brave I am ready for a cha
m here to experience life I am here to love others I am here to be lo
am gutsy I am afraid of lots of things I am curious I am an artist
am a lover of music I am a lover of dancing I am a lover of people
m breathing I am thinking I am wondering I am feeling I am talkir
am reinventing I am building I am creating I am dreaming I am pla
art of creation I am looking for awe I am noticing beauty I am a na
m starting over I am celebrating I am grieving I am cleaning up a bi
am loved I am misunderstood I am seen I am heard I am not done livir
full of life I am going through hard things right now I am having a
m lucky I am blessed I am learning to accept this time in my life I a
a free spirit I am unlearning I am remembering I am revisiting I am

Today I know what it feels like to:

Today I saw:

Today I am thinking about:

Today I heard:

Today I am feeling really good about:

Today I remembered:

Today I wish I could:

Today I learned:

ove who you are I see you you make a difference to me its okay to s
are doing a great job it's okay to rest you are learning so much
ave so much to be proud of and about you are magnificent there are
have what it takes you are acing this you are magnificent you ar
do this it's okay to ask for help you worked hard for this you are
can trust yourself miracles are meant for you too you are learning
e so much stronger than you think you are this will teach you things
ou can take the time you need you get to decide this is your life yo
i'll learn from this you will be more experienced on the other side of
nny you are fun you are so full of life you are the perfect one fo
ind what you are looking for you will never regret going on this adv
meant to enjoy this time in your life you can help others with your e
good you are true you are beautiful you are smart you are valu
i will get through this you will become the next version of yourself
t to start over you get to dream new dreams you get to make this wha
u get to reinvent yourself you get to let go of what no longer serves
e worth protecting you get to change you get to grow you get to evo
are phenomenal you are going to figure this out your life is worth
a gift you are worth the time you are a genius you are gorgeous
e my favorite you are the best you there ever was you are something
on your own path you are on your own journey you are getting thro
i matter in this world you are fun to be with you are enough in eve
re the real deal you are interesting you are doing a really good jo
e the one you are trustworthy you are always a big surprise you a
re one of a kind you are just as important as everyone else you get
ou are safe you are courageous you made it through you did it yo
to do what you want to do now you get to take the next step you get
i are kind you are a rare bird you are a beautiful soul you are sma
ou are part of this world you belong you are fun to be with you a
e a talented human you are on your way you are brave enough to do
re magical you have a beautiful heart you are a warrior you are w
u have the best ideas you worked hard for this you deserve every go
he strength to make it you can climb that mountain you can make it
re a miracle you are a masterpiece you are full of surprises you a
e style you are unique you are creative you can make it your own
can do this your own way you can make this your own you can put y
i are good hearted you are dependable you are full of strength yo
e made of love you have the best laugh you are thoughful you are
someone I admire you are someone to learn from you are a gift to th
e the one I want to be with you are the one I think about all the tim
are awesome you have a wild imagination you are pure and real yo

This is my beautiful life

I am learning from my experiences

Today I feel grateful	I am going for it
Today I feel sorrow	I am letting it go
Today I feel loved	I am ready for this
Today I feel amazing	I am a champion
Today feels so good	I am exhausted
Today I am surviving	I am so over this
Today I feel confused	I am so happy today
Today I feel courageous	I am having a good time
Today I am ending this	I am going to bed
Today I am beginning	I am celebrating this
Today I did something big	I am brave
Today I am disappointed	I am on my own path
Today I created this	I am an adventurer
Today I found this	I am learning this

cut here

ife is maddening life is exhilirating life is wierd life is phenome
an adventure life is more than what it seems life is changing lif
ife is good life is devastating life is chaotic life is precious l
is stressful life is restorative life is colorful life is dull li
magical life is about love life is about learning life is connect
ife will break you life will grow you life will teach you life wi
hallenge you life will ask you life will be relentless life will l
l make you what you are meant to be life will let you experience cons
oing life will soften you life will toughen you up life will retu
e does not give up on you life will patiently wait for you to learn
s gorgeous life is in order life is a paradox life is a mystery
ife is lovely life holds gifts for you life wants you to notice lif
not always fair life can transform pain into wisdom life is here to
t to be lived life is meant to be experienced life is meant to be enj
fe will not leave you behind life is on your side life will let you
mined life is amazing life is surprising life is difficult life is
life is educating life is transformative life is perplexing life i
ife is maddening life is exhilirating life is wierd life is phenome
an adventure life is more than what it seems life is changing lif
ife is good life is devastating life is chaotic life is precious l
is stressful life is restorative life is colorful life is dull li
magical life is about love life is about learning life is connect
ife will break you life will grow you life will teach you life wi
hallenge you life will ask you life will be relentless life will l
l make you what you are meant to be life will let you experience cons
oing life will soften you life will toughen you up life will retur
e does not give up on you life will patiently wait for you to learn
s gorgeous life is in order life is a paradox life is a mystery
ife is lovely life holds gifts for you life wants you to notice lif
not always fair life can transform pain into wisdom life is here to
t to be lived life is meant to be experienced life is meant to be enj
will not leave you behind life is on your side life will let you le
mined life is amazing life is surprising life is difficult life is
life is educating life is transformative life is perplexing life i
ife is maddening life is exhilirating life is wierd life is phenome
an adventure life is more than what it seems life is changing lif
ife is good life is devastating life is chaotic life is precious l
is stressful life is restorative life is colorful life is dull li
magical life is about love life is about learning life is connect
ife will break you life will grow you life will teach you life wi
hallenge you life will ask you life will be relentless life will l

Only I can change
my life. No one can
do it for me.

Carol Burnett

We must be willing
to let go of the life
we've planned,
so as to have the life
that is waiting for us.

Joseph Campbell

Look at life through
the windshield,
not the rear-view mirror.

Byrd Baggett

We can not become
what we need to be
by remaining what we are.

Oprah Winfrey

Life is not about waiting
for the storms to pass,
It's about learning how
to dance in the rain.

Vivian Greene

It takes courage
to grow up and become
who you really are.

E.E. Cummings

Life is a wild ride. . . . hold on tight.

Every experience brings you
a new piece of yourself.

cut here

am on my own path I am recovering I am getting stronger I am phen
n good at lots of things I am okay that I am not good at everything I
am full of awe I am ready for adventure I am on a mission I am a m
a letting go I am holding on tight I am figuring it out I am often c
m a soul I am a human being I am an individual I am part of it al
am letting myself begin again I am remembering the good things I have
I am a warrior I am a gentle heart I am brave I am ready for a cha
m here to experience life I am here to love others I am here to be lo
m gutsy I am afraid of lots of things I am curious I am an artist
am a lover of music I am a lover of dancing I am a lover of people
a breathing I am thinking I am wondering I am feeling I am talkir
am reinventing I am building I am creating I am dreaming I am pla
art of creation I am looking for awe I am noticing beauty I am a na
m starting over I am celebrating I am grieving I am cleaning up a bi
am loved I am misunderstood I am seen I am heard I am not done livir
full of life I am going through hard things right now I am having a
m lucky I am blessed I am learning to accept this time in my life I a
a free spirit I am unlearning I am remembering I am revisiting I am
m in love with the earth I am a lover of color I am a happy person I
nding up for what I believe in I am standing up for others I am doin
courageous I am working on my life I am focusing on self-respect I a
m powerful I am strong I am learning I am beautiful in my own wa
l I am alive I am a part of the human family I am beloved I am a m
am on my own path I am recovering I am getting stronger I am phen
n good at lots of things I am okay that I am not good at everything I
am full of awe I am ready for adventure I am on a mission I am a m
a letting go I am holding on tight I am figuring it out I am often c
m a soul I am a human being I am an individual I am part of it al
am letting myself begin again I am remembering the good things I have
I am a warrior I am a gentle heart I am brave I am ready for a cha
m here to experience life I am here to love others I am here to be lo
m gutsy I am afraid of lots of things I am curious I am an artist
am a lover of music I am a lover of dancing I am a lover of people
a breathing I am thinking I am wondering I am feeling I am talkir
am reinventing I am building I am creating I am dreaming I am pla
art of creation I am looking for awe I am noticing beauty I am a na
m starting over I am celebrating I am grieving I am cleaning up a bi
am loved I am misunderstood I am seen I am heard I am not done livir
full of life I am going through hard things right now I am having a
m lucky I am blessed I am learning to accept this time in my life I a
a free spirit I am unlearning I am remembering I am revisiting I am

REINVENT

ask
for
it

dream it

WORTH
IT

cultivate it

READY FOR A CHANGE

ove who you are   i see you   you make a difference to me   its okay to s
are doing a great job   it's okay to rest   you are learning so much
ave so much to be proud of and about   you are magnificent   there are
have what it takes   you are acing this   you are magnificent   you ar
do this   it's okay to ask for help   you worked hard for this   you are
can trust yourself   miracles are meant for you too   you are learning
e so much stronger than you think you are   this will teach you things
ou can take the time you need   you get to decide   this is your life   yo
ll learn from this   you will be more experienced on the other side of
nny   you are fun   you are so full of life   you are the perfect one fc
ind what you are looking for   you will never regret going on this adv
meant to enjoy this time in your life   you can help others with your e
good   you are true   you are beautiful   you are smart   you are valu
i will get through this   you will become the next version of yourself
t to start over   you get to dream new dreams   you get to make this wha
i get to reinvent yourself   you get to let go of what no longer serves
e worth protecting   you get to change   you get to grow   you get to evo
are phenomenal   you are going to figure this out   your life is worth
a gift   you are worth the time   you are a genius   you are gorgeous
e my favorite   you are the best you there ever was   you are something
on your own path   you are on your own journey   you are getting thro
i matter in this world   you are fun to be with   you are enough in eve
re the real deal   you are interesting   you are doing a really good jo
e the one   you are trustworthy   you are always a big surprise   you a
re one of a kind   you are just as important as everyone else   you get
ou are safe   you are courageous   you made it through   you did it   yo
to do what you want to do now   you get to take the next step   you get
i are kind   you are a rare bird   you are a beautiful soul   you are sm
ou are part of this world   you belong   you are fun to be with   you a
e a talented human   you are on your way   you are brave enough to do
re magical   you have a beautiful heart   you are a warrior   you are w
u have the best ideas   you worked hard for this   you deserve every go
he strength to make it   you can climb that mountain   you can make it
re a miracle   you are a masterpiece   you are full of surprises   you a
e style   you are unique   you are creative   you can make it your own
can do this your own way   you can make this your own   you can put y
i are good hearted   you are dependable   you are full of strength   yo
re made of love   you have the best laugh   you are thoughful   you are
someone I admire   you are someone to learn from   you are a gift to tl
e the one I want to be with   you are the one I think about all the tim
are awesome   you have a wild imagination   you are pure and real   yo

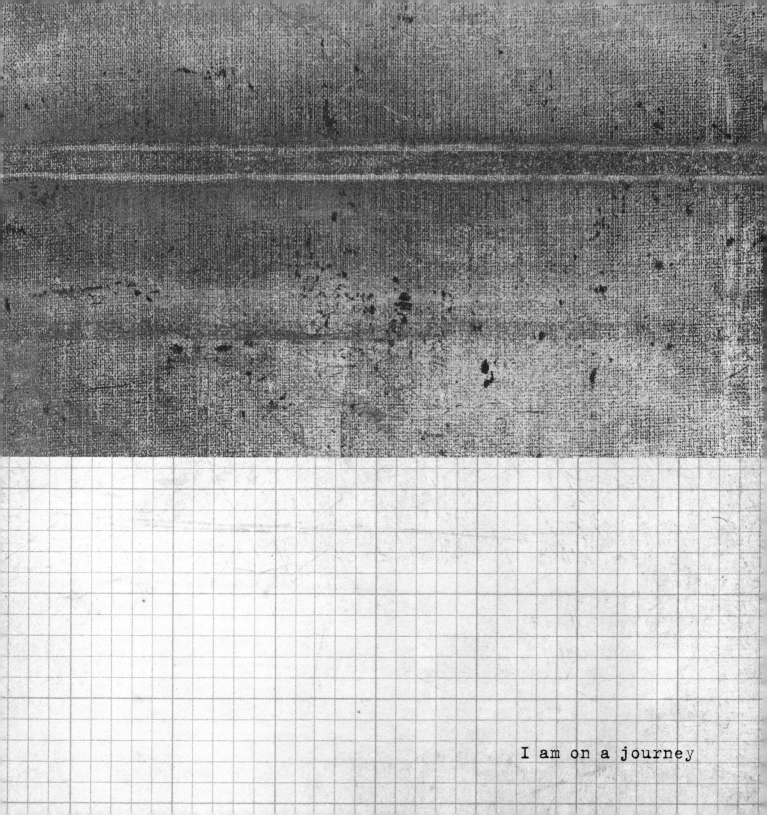

I am on a journey

fe is maddening life is exhilirating life is wierd life is phenome
an adventure life is more than what it seems life is changing lif
ife is good life is devastating life is chaotic life is precious l
is stressful life is restorative life is colorful life is dull li
magical life is about love life is about learning life is connect
ife will break you life will grow you life will teach you life wil
hallenge you life will ask you life will be relentless life will l
l make you what you are meant to be life will let you experience cons
oing life will soften you life will toughen you up life will retur
e does not give up on you life will patiently wait for you to learn
s gorgeous life is in order life is a paradox life is a mystery
ife is lovely life holds gifts for you life wants you to notice lif
not always fair life can transform pain into wisdom life is here to
t to be lived life is meant to be experienced life is meant to be enjo
fe will not leave you behind life is on your side life will let you
mined life is amazing life is surprising life is difficult life is
life is educating life is transformative life is perplexing life i
fe is maddening life is exhilirating life is wierd life is phenome
an adventure life is more than what it seems life is changing lif
ife is good life is devastating life is chaotic life is precious l
is stressful life is restorative life is colorful life is dull li
magical life is about love life is about learning life is connect
ife will break you life will grow you life will teach you life wil
hallenge you life will ask you life will be relentless life will l
l make you what you are meant to be life will let you experience cons
oing life will soften you life will toughen you up life will retur
e does not give up on you life will patiently wait for you to learn
s gorgeous life is in order life is a paradox life is a mystery
ife is lovely life holds gifts for you life wants you to notice lif
not always fair life can transform pain into wisdom life is here to
t to be lived life is meant to be experienced life is meant to be enj
will not leave you behind life is on your side life will let you le
mined life is amazing life is surprising life is difficult life is
life is educating life is transformative life is perplexing life i
ife is maddening life is exhilirating life is wierd life is phenome
an adventure life is more than what it seems life is changing lif
ife is good life is devastating life is chaotic life is precious l
is stressful life is restorative life is colorful life is dull li
magical life is about love life is about learning life is connect
ife will break you life will grow you life will teach you life wil
hallenge you life will ask you life will be relentless life will l

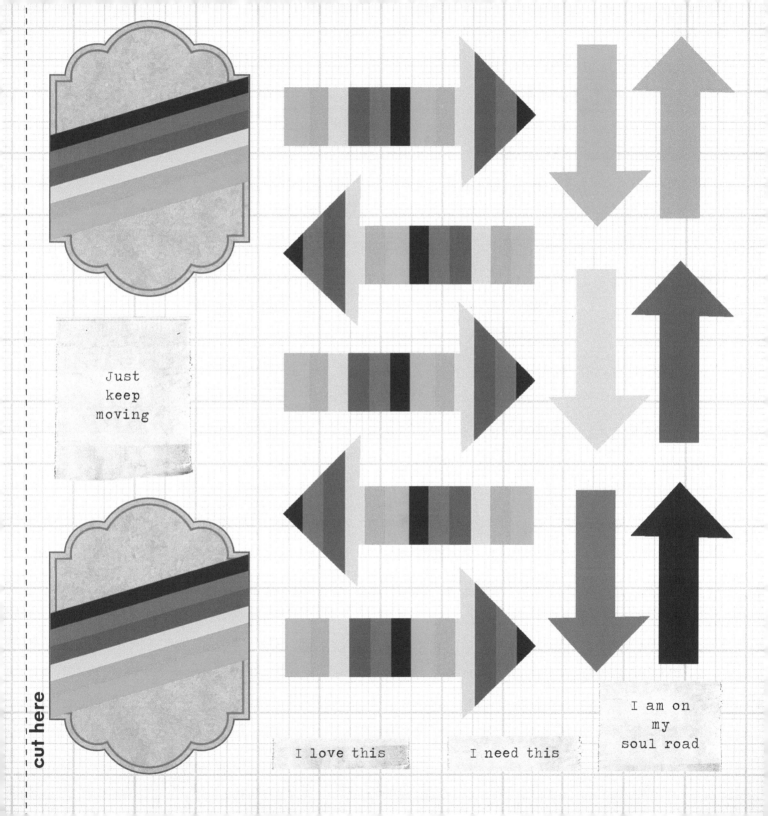

cut here

Just
keep
moving

I love this

I need this

I am on
my
soul road

am on my own path I am recovering I am getting stronger I am phen
n good at lots of things I am okay that I am not good at everything I
am full of awe I am ready for adventure I am on a mission I am a m
n letting go I am holding on tight I am figuring it out I am often c
m a soul I am a human being I am an individual I am part of it al
am letting myself begin again I am remembering the good things I have
I am a warrior I am a gentle heart I am brave I am ready for a cha
m here to experience life I am here to love others I am here to be lo
m gutsy I am afraid of lots of things I am curious I am an artist
am a lover of music I am a lover of dancing I am a lover of people I
n breathing I am thinking I am wondering I am feeling I am talkin
am reinventing I am building I am creating I am dreaming I am pla
art of creation I am looking for awe I am noticing beauty I am a na
m starting over I am celebrating I am grieving I am cleaning up a bi
am loved I am misunderstood I am seen I am heard I am not done livin
full of life I am going through hard things right now I am having a
m lucky I am blessed I am learning to accept this time in my life I a
a free spirit I am unlearning I am remembering I am revisiting I am
n in love with the earth I am a lover of color I am a happy person I
nding up for what I believe in I am standing up for others I am doin
courageous I am working on my life I am focusing on self-respect I a
m powerful I am strong I am learning I am beautiful in my own wa
l I am alive I am a part of the human family I am beloved I am a m
am on my own path I am recovering I am getting stronger I am phen
n good at lots of things I am okay that I am not good at everything I
am full of awe I am ready for adventure I am on a mission I am a m
n letting go I am holding on tight I am figuring it out I am often c
m a soul I am a human being I am an individual I am part of it al
am letting myself begin again I am remembering the good things I have
I am a warrior I am a gentle heart I am brave I am ready for a cha
m here to experience life I am here to love others I am here to be lo
am gutsy I am afraid of lots of things I am curious I am an artist
am a lover of music I am a lover of dancing I am a lover of people I
n breathing I am thinking I am wondering I am feeling I am talkin
am reinventing I am building I am creating I am dreaming I am pla
art of creation I am looking for awe I am noticing beauty I am a na
m starting over I am celebrating I am grieving I am cleaning up a bi
am loved I am misunderstood I am seen I am heard I am not done livin
full of life I am going through hard things right now I am having a
m lucky I am blessed I am learning to accept this time in my life I a
a free spirit I am unlearning I am remembering I am revisiting I am

I am still becoming

What a wild ride this life is

cut here

Things that matter to me:

1.

2.

3.

I am still
becoming

ove who you are i see you you make a difference to me its okay to s
i are doing a great job it's okay to rest you are learning so much
ave so much to be proud of and about you are magnificent there are
have what it takes you are acing this you are magnificent you ar
do this it's okay to ask for help you worked hard for this you are
can trust yourself miracles are meant for you too you are learning
e so much stronger than you think you are this will teach you things
ou can take the time you need you get to decide this is your life yo
i'll learn from this you will be more experienced on the other side of
nny you are fun you are so full of life you are the perfect one fo
ind what you are looking for you will never regret going on this adv
meant to enjoy this time in your life you can help others with your e
good you are true you are beautiful you are smart you are valu
i will get through this you will become the next version of yourself
t to start over you get to dream new dreams you get to make this wha
u get to reinvent yourself you get to let go of what no longer serves
e worth protecting you get to change you get to grow you get to evo
are phenomenal you are going to figure this out your life is worth
a gift you are worth the time you are a genius you are gorgeous
e my favorite you are the best you there ever was you are something
on your own path you are on your own journey you are getting thro
i matter in this world you are fun to be with you are enough in eve
re the real deal you are interesting you are doing a really good jo
e the one you are trustworthy you are always a big surprise you a
re one of a kind you are just as important as everyone else you get
u are safe you are courageous you made it through you did it yo
to do what you want to do now you get to take the next step you get
i are kind you are a rare bird you are a beautiful soul you are sma
u are part of this world you belong you are fun to be with you a
e a talented human you are on your way you are brave enough to do
re magical you have a beautiful heart you are a warrior you are w
u have the best ideas you worked hard for this you deserve every go
he strength to make it you can climb that mountain you can make it
re a miracle you are a masterpiece you are full of surprises you a
e style you are unique you are creative you can make it your own
can do this your own way you can make this your own you can put y
i are good hearted you are dependable you are full of strength yo
re made of love you have the best laugh you are thoughful you are
someone I admire you are someone to learn from you are a gift to th
e the one I want to be with you are the one I think about all the tim
are awesome you have a wild imagination you are pure and real yo

cut here

believe in miracles

notice the little things

grow your wings

make time for living

ife is maddening life is exhilirating life is wierd life is phenome
an adventure life is more than what it seems life is changing lif
life is good life is devastating life is chaotic life is precious l
is stressful life is restorative life is colorful life is dull li
magical life is about love life is about learning life is connect
life will break you life will grow you life will teach you life wil
hallenge you life will ask you life will be relentless life will l
l make you what you are meant to be life will let you experience cons
oing life will soften you life will toughen you up life will retur
e does not give up on you life will patiently wait for you to learn
s gorgeous life is in order life is a paradox life is a mystery
ife is lovely life holds gifts for you life wants you to notice lif
not always fair life can transform pain into wisdom life is here to
t to be lived life is meant to be experienced life is meant to be enj
fe will not leave you behind life is on your side life will let you
mined life is amazing life is surprising life is difficult life is
life is educating life is transformative life is perplexing life i
ife is maddening life is exhilirating life is wierd life is phenome
an adventure life is more than what it seems life is changing lif
ife is good life is devastating life is chaotic life is precious l
is stressful life is restorative life is colorful life is dull li
magical life is about love life is about learning life is connect
ife will break you life will grow you life will teach you life wil
hallenge you life will ask you life will be relentless life will l
l make you what you are meant to be life will let you experience cons
oing life will soften you life will toughen you up life will retur
e does not give up on you life will patiently wait for you to learn
s gorgeous life is in order life is a paradox life is a mystery
ife is lovely life holds gifts for you life wants you to notice lif
not always fair life can transform pain into wisdom life is here to
t to be lived life is meant to be experienced life is meant to be enj
will not leave you behind life is on your side life will let you le
mined life is amazing life is surprising life is difficult life is
life is educating life is transformative life is perplexing life i
ife is maddening life is exhilirating life is wierd life is phenome
an adventure life is more than what it seems life is changing lif
ife is good life is devastating life is chaotic life is precious l
is stressful life is restorative life is colorful life is dull li
magical life is about love life is about learning life is connect
ife will break you life will grow you life will teach you life wil
hallenge you life will ask you life will be relentless life will l

There is always something to be thankful for

I am ready to do something brave and life-changing

I am free

be gutsy

cut here

am on my own path I am recovering I am getting stronger I am phe
n good at lots of things I am okay that I am not good at everything I
am full of awe I am ready for adventure I am on a mission I am a
n letting go I am holding on tight I am figuring it out I am often
m a soul I am a human being I am an individual I am part of it a
am letting myself begin again I am remembering the good things I hav
I am a warrior I am a gentle heart I am brave I am ready for a ch
m here to experience life I am here to love others I am here to be l
m gutsy I am afraid of lots of things I am curious I am an artist
am a lover of music I am a lover of dancing I am a lover of people
n breathing I am thinking I am wondering I am feeling I am talki
am reinventing I am building I am creating I am dreaming I am p
art of creation I am looking for awe I am noticing beauty I am a n
m starting over I am celebrating I am grieving I am cleaning up a
am loved I am misunderstood I am seen I am heard I am not done livi
full of life I am going through hard things right now I am having a
n lucky I am blessed I am learning to accept this time in my life I
a free spirit I am unlearning I am remembering I am revisiting I a
n in love with the earth I am a lover of color I am a happy person I
nding up for what I believe in I am standing up for others I am doi
courageous I am working on my life I am focusing on self-respect I
m powerful I am strong I am learning I am beautiful in my own wa
l I am alive I am a part of the human family I am beloved I am a
am on my own path I am recovering I am getting stronger I am phe

n good at lots of things I am okay that I am not good at everything I
am full of awe I am ready for adventure I am on a mission I am a
n letting go I am holding on tight I am figuring it out I am often
m a soul I am a human being I am an individual I am part of it a
am letting myself begin again I am remembering the good things I hav
I am a warrior I am a gentle heart I am brave I am ready for a ch
m here to experience life I am here to love others I am here to be l
am gutsy I am afraid of lots of things I am curious I am an artist
am a lover of music I am a lover of dancing I am a lover of people
n breathing I am thinking I am wondering I am feeling I am talki
am reinventing I am building I am creating I am dreaming I am p
art of creation I am looking for awe I am noticing beauty I am a n
m starting over I am celebrating I am grieving I am cleaning up a
am loved I am misunderstood I am seen I am heard I am not done livi
full of life I am going through hard things right now I am having a
n lucky I am blessed I am learning to accept this time in my life I
a free spirit I am unlearning I am remembering I am revisiting I a

What impacted me the most about this experience?

What would I change about this if I could?

What did I see that I had never seen before?

Who did I meet because this happened?

What is something I never want to forget?

How did all of this happen this way?

What am I hoping will happen next?

What is my overall feeling about this experience?

Who helped to make this happen?

What were some of the surprises along the way?

What part do I hope to never have to experience again?

What part of this makes me giddy when I think about it?

What part of this makes me cry when I think about it?

What will I do differently next time?

Who did I learn the most from during this time?

What surrounded me while all of this was going on?

How did my goals change after this?

What would I do exactly the same because it worked so well?

What role did I play in this experience?

cut here

ve who you are I see you you make a difference to me it's okay to
are doing a great job it's okay to rest you are learning so much
ave so much to be proud of and about you are magnificent there are
have what it takes you are acing this you are magnificent you ar
do this it's okay to ask for help you worked hard for this you are
can trust yourself miracles are meant for you too you are learning
e so much stronger than you think you are this will teach you things
u can take the time you need you get to decide this is your life yo
'll learn from this you will be more experienced on the other side of
ny you are fun you are so full of life you are the perfect one fo
ind what you are looking for you will never regret going on this adv
meant to enjoy this time in your life you can help others with your e
good you are true you are beautiful you are smart you are valu
l will get through this you will become the next version of yourself
t to start over you get to dream new dreams you get to make this wha
l get to reinvent yourself you get to let go of what no longer serves
e worth protecting you get to change you get to grow you get to evo
re phenomenal you are going to figure this out your life is worth
a gift you are worth the time you are a genius you are gorgeous
e my favorite you are the best you there ever was you are something
on your own path you are on your own journey you are getting thro
u matter in this world you are fun to be with you are enough in eve
re the real deal you are interesting you are doing a really good jo
the one you are trustworthy you are always a big surprise you a
re one of a kind you are just as important as everyone else you get
u are safe you are courageous you made it through you did it yo
to do what you want to do now you get to take the next step you get
u are kind you are a rare bird you are a beautiful soul you are sma
u are part of this world you belong you are fun to be with you a
e a talented human you are on your way you are brave enough to do
re magical you have a beautiful heart you are a warrior you are w
u have the best ideas you worked hard for this you deserve every go
he strength to make it you can climb that mountain you can make it
re a miracle you are a masterpiece you are full of surprises you a
e style you are unique you are creative you can make it your own
can do this your own way you can make this your own you can put y
u are good hearted you are dependable you are full of strength yo
e made of love you have the best laugh you are thoughful you are
someone I admire you are someone to learn from you are a gift to th
e the one I want to be with you are the one I think about all the tim
are awesome you have a wild imagination you are pure and real yo

HELLO LIFE

I am learning and growing

fe is maddening life is exhilirating life is wierd life is phenome
an adventure life is more than what it seems life is changing life
life is good life is devastating life is chaotic life is precious l
is stressful life is restorative life is colorful life is dull li
magical life is about love life is about learning life is connect
ife will break you life will grow you life will teach you life wil
hallenge you life will ask you life will be relentless life will l
l make you what you are meant to be life will let you experience cons
oing life will soften you life will toughen you up life will retur
e does not give up on you life will patiently wait for you to learn
s gorgeous life is in order life is a paradox life is a mystery
ife is lovely life holds gifts for you life wants you to notice lif
not always fair life can transform pain into wisdom life is here to
t to be lived life is meant to be experienced life is meant to be enj
fe will not leave you behind life is on your side life will let you
mined life is amazing life is surprising life is difficult life is
life is educating life is transformative life is perplexing life i
fe is maddening life is exhilirating life is wierd life is phenome
an adventure life is more than what it seems life is changing life
ife is good life is devastating life is chaotic life is precious l
is stressful life is restorative life is colorful life is dull li
magical life is about love life is about learning life is connect
ife will break you life will grow you life will teach you life wil
hallenge you life will ask you life will be relentless life will l
l make you what you are meant to be life will let you experience cons
oing life will soften you life will toughen you up life will retur
e does not give up on you life will patiently wait for you to learn
s gorgeous life is in order life is a paradox life is a mystery
ife is lovely life holds gifts for you life wants you to notice lif
not always fair life can transform pain into wisdom life is here to
t to be lived life is meant to be experienced life is meant to be enj
will not leave you behind life is on your side life will let you le
mined life is amazing life is surprising life is difficult life is
life is educating life is transformative life is perplexing life i
fe is maddening life is exhilirating life is wierd life is phenome
an adventure life is more than what it seems life is changing life
ife is good life is devastating life is chaotic life is precious l
is stressful life is restorative life is colorful life is dull li
magical life is about love life is about learning life is connect
ife will break you life will grow you life will teach you life wil
hallenge you life will ask you life will be relentless life will l

cut here

FLY

I have to be free

am on my own path I am recovering I am getting stronger I am phen
good at lots of things I am okay that I am not good at everything I
am full of awe I am ready for adventure I am on a mission I am a m
letting go I am holding on tight I am figuring it out I am often c
m a soul I am a human being I am an individual I am part of it al
am letting myself begin again I am remembering the good things I have
I am a warrior I am a gentle heart I am brave I am ready for a cha
m here to experience life I am here to love others I am here to be lo
m gutsy I am afraid of lots of things I am curious I am an artist
am a lover of music I am a lover of dancing I am a lover of people
breathing I am thinking I am wondering I am feeling I am talkir
am reinventing I am building I am creating I am dreaming I am pla
art of creation I am looking for awe I am noticing beauty I am a na
m starting over I am celebrating I am grieving I am cleaning up a bi
am loved I am misunderstood I am seen I am heard I am not done livir
full of life I am going through hard things right now I am having a
n lucky I am blessed I am learning to accept this time in my life I a
a free spirit I am unlearning I am remembering I am revisiting I am
n in love with the earth I am a lover of color I am a happy person I
nding up for what I believe in I am standing up for others I am doin
courageous I am working on my life I am focusing on self-respect I a
m powerful I am strong I am learning I am beautiful in my own wa
l I am alive I am a part of the human family I am beloved I am a m
am on my own path I am recovering I am getting stronger I am phen
good at lots of things I am okay that I am not good at everything I
am full of awe I am ready for adventure I am on a mission I am a m
letting go I am holding on tight I am figuring it out I am often c
m a soul I am a human being I am an individual I am part of it al
am letting myself begin again I am remembering the good things I have
I am a warrior I am a gentle heart I am brave I am ready for a cha
m here to experience life I am here to love others I am here to be lo
m gutsy I am afraid of lots of things I am curious I am an artist
am a lover of music I am a lover of dancing I am a lover of people
breathing I am thinking I am wondering I am feeling I am talkir
am reinventing I am building I am creating I am dreaming I am pla
art of creation I am looking for awe I am noticing beauty I am a na
m starting over I am celebrating I am grieving I am cleaning up a bi
am loved I am misunderstood I am seen I am heard I am not done livir
full of life I am going through hard things right now I am having a
n lucky I am blessed I am learning to accept this time in my life I a
a free spirit I am unlearning I am remembering I am revisiting I am

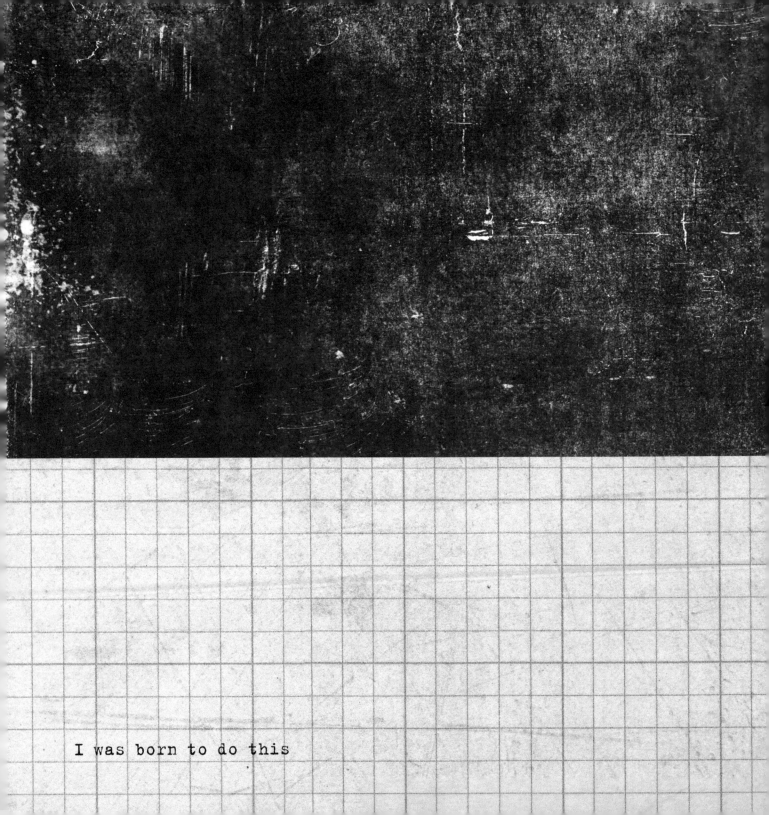

I was born to do this

I prefer

Happiness is

Everyone knows

Watch out for

You'll find me

The secret is

We know how to

It is time to

cut here

ve who you are i see you you make a difference to me its okay to s
are doing a great job it's okay to rest you are learning so much
ave so much to be proud of and about you are magnificent there are
have what it takes you are acing this you are magnificent you ar
do this it's okay to ask for help you worked hard for this you are
can trust yourself miracles are meant for you too you are learning
e so much stronger than you think you are this will teach you things
u can take the time you need you get to decide this is your life yo
ll learn from this you will be more experienced on the other side of
ny you are fun you are so full of life you are the perfect one fo
ind what you are looking for you will never regret going on this adv
meant to enjoy this time in your life you can help others with your e
good you are true you are beautiful you are smart you are valu
i will get through this you will become the next version of yourself
t to start over you get to dream new dreams you get to make this wha
u get to reinvent yourself you get to let go of what no longer serves
e worth protecting you get to change you get to grow you get to evo
are phenomenal you are going to figure this out your life is worth
a gift you are worth the time you are a genius you are gorgeous
e my favorite you are the best you there ever was you are something
on your own path you are on your own journey you are getting thro
u matter in this world you are fun to be with you are enough in eve
re the real deal you are interesting you are doing a really good jo
the one you are trustworthy you are always a big surprise you a
re one of a kind you are just as important as everyone else you get
u are safe you are courageous you made it through you did it yo
to do what you want to do now you get to take the next step you get
u are kind you are a rare bird you are a beautiful soul you are sma
u are part of this world you belong you are fun to be with you a
e a talented human you are on your way you are brave enough to do
re magical you have a beautiful heart you are a warrior you are w
u have the best ideas you worked hard for this you deserve every go
he strength to make it you can climb that mountain you can make it
re a miracle you are a masterpiece you are full of surprises you a
e style you are unique you are creative you can make it your own
can do this your own way you can make this your own you can put y
u are good hearted you are dependable you are full of strength yo
re made of love you have the best laugh you are thoughful you are
someone I admire you are someone to learn from you are a gift to th
e the one I want to be with you are the one I think about all the tim
are awesome you have a wild imagination you are pure and real yo

.fe is maddening life is exhilirating life is wierd life is phenome
an adventure life is more than what it seems life is changing lif
life is good life is devastating life is chaotic life is precious 1
is stressful life is restorative life is colorful life is dull li
magical life is about love life is about learning life is connect
ife will break you life will grow you life will teach you life wil
hallenge you life will ask you life will be relentless life will l
l make you what you are meant to be life will let you experience cons
oing life will soften you life will toughen you up life will retur
e does not give up on you life will patiently wait for you to learn
s gorgeous life is in order life is a paradox life is a mystery
ife is lovely life holds gifts for you life wants you to notice lif
not always fair life can transform pain into wisdom life is here to
t to be lived life is meant to be experienced life is meant to be enj
fe will not leave you behind life is on your side life will let you
mined life is amazing life is surprising life is difficult life is
life is educating life is transformative life is perplexing life i
ife is maddening life is exhilirating life is wierd life is phenome
an adventure life is more than what it seems life is changing lif
ife is good life is devastating life is chaotic life is precious 1
is stressful life is restorative life is colorful life is dull li
magical life is about love life is about learning life is connect
ife will break you life will grow you life will teach you life wil
hallenge you life will ask you life will be relentless life will l
l make you what you are meant to be life will let you experience cons
oing life will soften you life will toughen you up life will retur
e does not give up on you life will patiently wait for you to learn
s gorgeous life is in order life is a paradox life is a mystery
ife is lovely life holds gifts for you life wants you to notice lif
not always fair life can transform pain into wisdom life is here to
t to be lived life is meant to be experienced life is meant to be enj
will not leave you behind life is on your side life will let you le
mined life is amazing life is surprising life is difficult life is
life is educating life is transformative life is perplexing life i
ife is maddening life is exhilirating life is wierd life is phenome
an adventure life is more than what it seems life is changing lif
ife is good life is devastating life is chaotic life is precious 1
is stressful life is restorative life is colorful life is dull li
magical life is about love life is about learning life is connect
life will break you life will grow you life will teach you life wil
hallenge you life will ask you life will be relentless life will l

Head toward the life you most want to live

I am more than what can be seen

cut here

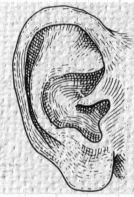

FAVORITE THINGS TO TASTE:

1.

2.

3.

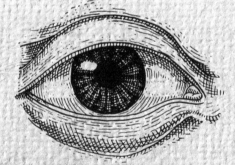

FAVORITE THINGS TO HEAR:

1.

2.

3.

FAVORITE THINGS TO SEE:

1.

2.

3.

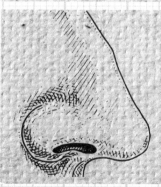

FAVORITE THINGS TO SMELL:

1.

2.

3.

am on my own path I am recovering I am getting stronger I am phen
n good at lots of things I am okay that I am not good at everything I
am full of awe I am ready for adventure I am on a mission I am a m
n letting go I am holding on tight I am figuring it out I am often c
m a soul I am a human being I am an individual I am part of it al
am letting myself begin again I am remembering the good things I have
I am a warrior I am a gentle heart I am brave I am ready for a cha
m here to experience life I am here to love others I am here to be lo
am gutsy I am afraid of lots of things I am curious I am an artist
am a lover of music I am a lover of dancing I am a lover of people
n breathing I am thinking I am wondering I am feeling I am talkir
am reinventing I am building I am creating I am dreaming I am pla
art of creation I am looking for awe I am noticing beauty I am a na
m starting over I am celebrating I am grieving I am cleaning up a bi
am loved I am misunderstood I am seen I am heard I am not done livir
full of life I am going through hard things right now I am having a
m lucky I am blessed I am learning to accept this time in my life I a
a free spirit I am unlearning I am remembering I am revisiting I am
n in love with the earth I am a lover of color I am a happy person I
nding up for what I believe in I am standing up for others I am doin
courageous I am working on my life I am focusing on self-respect I a
m powerful I am strong I am learning I am beautiful in my own wa
l I am alive I am a part of the human family I am beloved I am a m
am on my own path I am recovering I am getting stronger I am phen
n good at lots of things I am okay that I am not good at everything I
am full of awe I am ready for adventure I am on a mission I am a m
n letting go I am holding on tight I am figuring it out I am often c
m a soul I am a human being I am an individual I am part of it al
am letting myself begin again I am remembering the good things I have
I am a warrior I am a gentle heart I am brave I am ready for a cha
m here to experience life I am here to love others I am here to be lo
am gutsy I am afraid of lots of things I am curious I am an artist
am a lover of music I am a lover of dancing I am a lover of people
n breathing I am thinking I am wondering I am feeling I am talkir
am reinventing I am building I am creating I am dreaming I am pla
art of creation I am looking for awe I am noticing beauty I am a na
m starting over I am celebrating I am grieving I am cleaning up a bi
am loved I am misunderstood I am seen I am heard I am not done livir
full of life I am going through hard things right now I am having a
m lucky I am blessed I am learning to accept this time in my life I a
a free spirit I am unlearning I am remembering I am revisiting I am

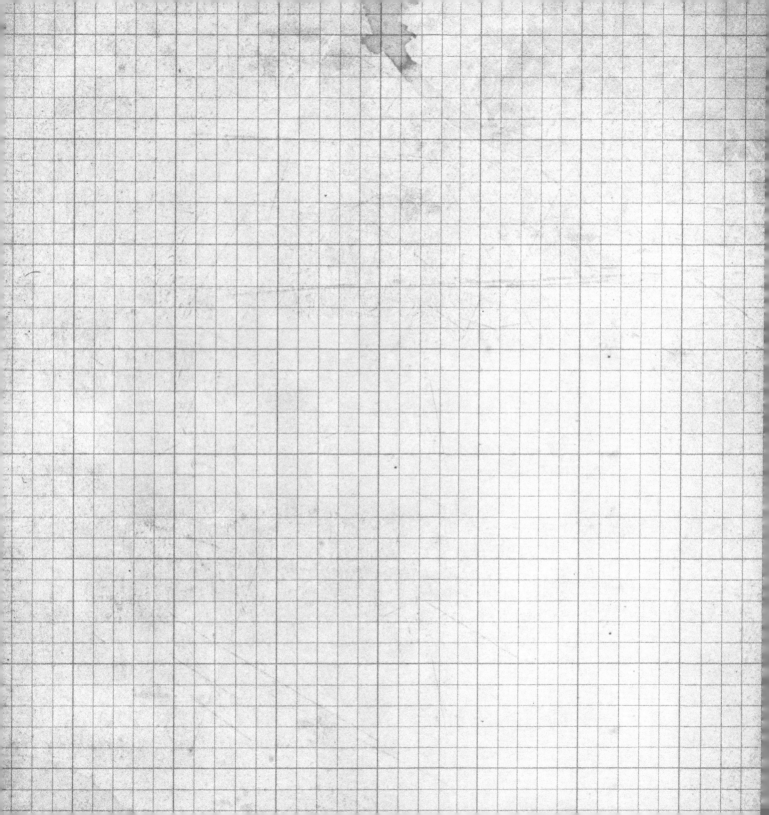

more fun please

I still believe in love.

Today is a perfect day to begin again.

brave chick

sing your own song

cut here

ove who you are i see you you make a difference to me its okay to s
i are doing a great job it's okay to rest you are learning so much
ave so much to be proud of and about you are magnificent there are
have what it takes you are acing this you are magnificent you ar
do this it's okay to ask for help you worked hard for this you are
can trust yourself miracles are meant for you too you are learning
e so much stronger than you think you are this will teach you things
u can take the time you need you get to decide this is your life yo
ll learn from this you will be more experienced on the other side of
nny you are fun you are so full of life you are the perfect one fo
ind what you are looking for you will never regret going on this adv
meant to enjoy this time in your life you can help others with your e
good you are true you are beautiful you are smart you are valu
i will get through this you will become the next version of yourself
t to start over you get to dream new dreams you get to make this wha
i get to reinvent yourself you get to let go of what no longer serves
e worth protecting you get to change you get to grow you get to evo
are phenomenal you are going to figure this out your life is worth
a gift you are worth the time you are a genius you are gorgeous
e my favorite you are the best you there ever was you are something
on your own path you are on your own journey you are getting thro
i matter in this world you are fun to be with you are enough in eve
re the real deal you are interesting you are doing a really good jo
e the one you are trustworthy you are always a big surprise you a
re one of a kind you are just as important as everyone else you get
u are safe you are courageous you made it through you did it yo
to do what you want to do now you get to take the next step you get
i are kind you are a rare bird you are a beautiful soul you are sma
u are part of this world you belong you are fun to be with you a
e a talented human you are on your way you are brave enough to do
re magical you have a beautiful heart you are a warrior you are w
u have the best ideas you worked hard for this you deserve every go
he strength to make it you can climb that mountain you can make it
re a miracle you are a masterpiece you are full of surprises you a
e style you are unique you are creative you can make it your own
can do this your own way you can make this your own you can put y
i are good hearted you are dependable you are full of strength yo
re made of love you have the best laugh you are thoughful you are
someone I admire you are someone to learn from you are a gift to th
e the one I want to be with you are the one I think about all the time
are awesome you have a wild imagination you are pure and real yo

I love my life

I would love to know what it's like to:

I have loved pretty much every moment of:

I usually go to sleep thinking about:

I would love to try to get really good at:

A word that describes the last year:

cut here

fe is maddening life is exhilirating life is wierd life is phenome
an adventure life is more than what it seems life is changing life
life is good life is devastating life is chaotic life is precious l
is stressful life is restorative life is colorful life is dull li
magical life is about love life is about learning life is connect
ife will break you life will grow you life will teach you life wil
hallenge you life will ask you life will be relentless life will l
l make you what you are meant to be life will let you experience cons
oing life will soften you life will toughen you up life will retur
e does not give up on you life will patiently wait for you to learn
s gorgeous life is in order life is a paradox life is a mystery
ife is lovely life holds gifts for you life wants you to notice lif
not always fair life can transform pain into wisdom life is here to
t to be lived life is meant to be experienced life is meant to be enj
fe will not leave you behind life is on your side life will let you
mined life is amazing life is surprising life is difficult life is
life is educating life is transformative life is perplexing life i
ife is maddening life is exhilirating life is wierd life is phenome
an adventure life is more than what it seems life is changing life
ife is good life is devastating life is chaotic life is precious l
is stressful life is restorative life is colorful life is dull li
magical life is about love life is about learning life is connect
ife will break you life will grow you life will teach you life wil
hallenge you life will ask you life will be relentless life will l
l make you what you are meant to be life will let you experience cons
oing life will soften you life will toughen you up life will retur
e does not give up on you life will patiently wait for you to learn
s gorgeous life is in order life is a paradox life is a mystery
ife is lovely life holds gifts for you life wants you to notice lif
not always fair life can transform pain into wisdom life is here to
t to be lived life is meant to be experienced life is meant to be enj
will not leave you behind life is on your side life will let you le
mined life is amazing life is surprising life is difficult life is
life is educating life is transformative life is perplexing life i
ife is maddening life is exhilirating life is wierd life is phenome
an adventure life is more than what it seems life is changing life
ife is good life is devastating life is chaotic life is precious l
is stressful life is restorative life is colorful life is dull li
magical life is about love life is about learning life is connect
ife will break you life will grow you life will teach you life wil
hallenge you life will ask you life will be relentless life will l

I am on my way

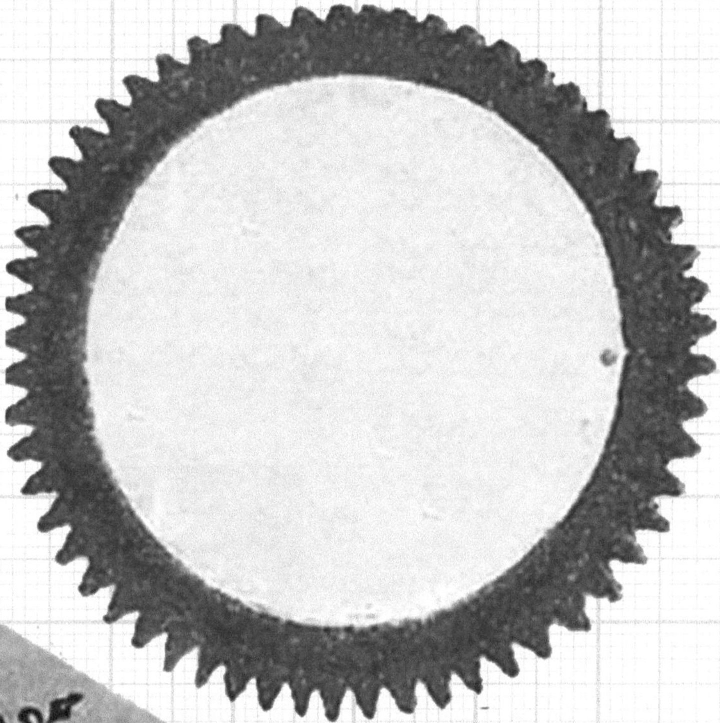

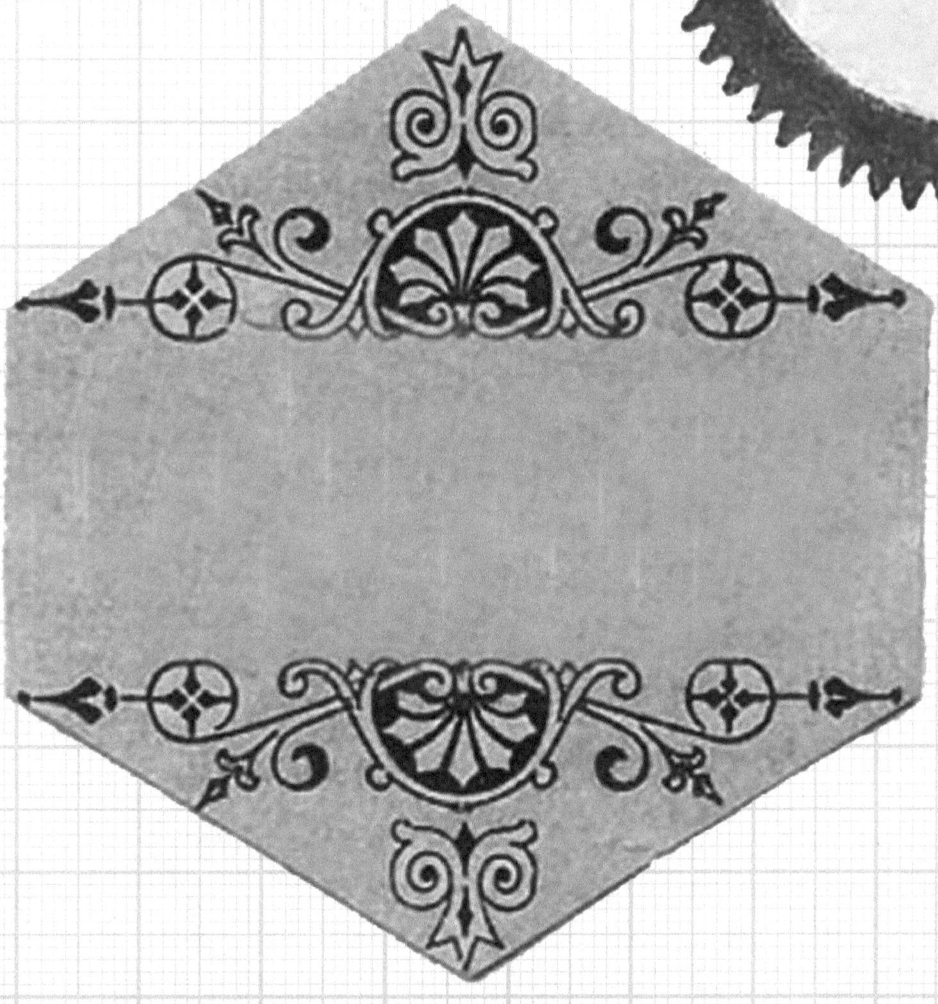

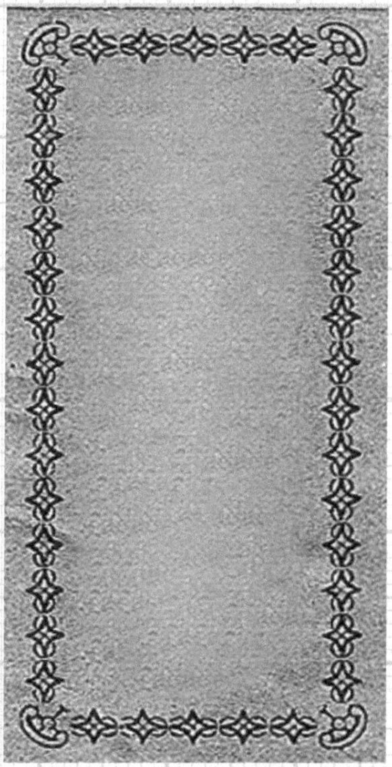

cut here

am on my own path I am recovering I am getting stronger I am phen
n good at lots of things I am okay that I am not good at everything I
am full of awe I am ready for adventure I am on a mission I am a m
n letting go I am holding on tight I am figuring it out I am often c
m a soul I am a human being I am an individual I am part of it al
am letting myself begin again I am remembering the good things I have
I am a warrior I am a gentle heart I am brave I am ready for a cha
m here to experience life I am here to love others I am here to be lo
am gutsy I am afraid of lots of things I am curious I am an artist
am a lover of music I am a lover of dancing I am a lover of people
n breathing I am thinking I am wondering I am feeling I am talkin
am reinventing I am building I am creating I am dreaming I am pla
art of creation I am looking for awe I am noticing beauty I am a na
m starting over I am celebrating I am grieving I am cleaning up a b
am loved I am misunderstood I am seen I am heard I am not done livin
full of life I am going through hard things right now I am having a
m lucky I am blessed I am learning to accept this time in my life I a
a free spirit I am unlearning I am remembering I am revisiting I am
n in love with the earth I am a lover of color I am a happy person I
nding up for what I believe in I am standing up for others I am doin
courageous I am working on my life I am focusing on self-respect I a
m powerful I am strong I am learning I am beautiful in my own wa
l I am alive I am a part of the human family I am beloved I am a m

am on my own path I am recovering I am getting stronger I am phen
n good at lots of things I am okay that I am not good at everything I
am full of awe I am ready for adventure I am on a mission I am a m
n letting go I am holding on tight I am figuring it out I am often c
m a soul I am a human being I am an individual I am part of it al
am letting myself begin again I am remembering the good things I have
I am a warrior I am a gentle heart I am brave I am ready for a cha
m here to experience life I am here to love others I am here to be lo
am gutsy I am afraid of lots of things I am curious I am an artist
am a lover of music I am a lover of dancing I am a lover of people
n breathing I am thinking I am wondering I am feeling I am talkin
am reinventing I am building I am creating I am dreaming I am pla
art of creation I am looking for awe I am noticing beauty I am a na
m starting over I am celebrating I am grieving I am cleaning up a b
am loved I am misunderstood I am seen I am heard I am not done livin
full of life I am going through hard things right now I am having a
m lucky I am blessed I am learning to accept this time in my life I a
a free spirit I am unlearning I am remembering I am revisiting I am

I will never forget this day	I love this person so much
This is who I am	It's time to do this
I need more of this	I learned so much
I am overcoming	Doing it anyway
A dream come true	Doing what it takes
I am proud of myself	Here we go again
I finally got here	I am dreaming of this
Let's do something fun	So happy together
My kind of road trip	My kind of happiness
All the feels	It took my breath away

cut here

ove who you are I see you you make a difference to me its okay to s
i are doing a great job it's okay to rest you are learning so much
ave so much to be proud of and about you are magnificent there are
have what it takes you are acing this you are magnificent you ar
do this it's okay to ask for help you worked hard for this you are
can trust yourself miracles are meant for you too you are learning
e so much stronger than you think you are this will teach you things
iu can take the time you need you get to decide this is your life yo
i'll learn from this you will be more experienced on the other side of
iny you are fun you are so full of life you are the perfect one fo
ind what you are looking for you will never regret going on this adv
meant to enjoy this time in your life you can help others with your e
good you are true you are beautiful you are smart you are valu
i will get through this you will become the next version of yourself
t to start over you get to dream new dreams you get to make this wha
i get to reinvent yourself you get to let go of what no longer serves
e worth protecting you get to change you get to grow you get to evo
ire phenomenal you are going to figure this out your life is worth
a gift you are worth the time you are a genius you are gorgeous
e my favorite you are the best you there ever was you are something
on your own path you are on your own journey you are getting thro
i matter in this world you are fun to be with you are enough in eve
re the real deal you are interesting you are doing a really good jo
the one you are trustworthy you are always a big surprise you a
re one of a kind you are just as important as everyone else you get
iu are safe you are courageous you made it through you did it yo
to do what you want to do now you get to take the next step you get
i are kind you are a rare bird you are a beautiful soul you are sma
iu are part of this world you belong you are fun to be with you a
e a talented human you are on your way you are brave enough to do
re magical you have a beautiful heart you are a warrior you are w
u have the best ideas you worked hard for this you deserve every go
he strength to make it you can climb that mountain you can make it
re a miracle you are a masterpiece you are full of surprises you a
e style you are unique you are creative you can make it your own
can do this your own way you can make this your own you can put y
i are good hearted you are dependable you are full of strength yo
e made of love you have the best laugh you are thoughful you are
someone I admire you are someone to learn from you are a gift to t
e the one I want to be with you are the one I think about all the tim
are awesome you have a wild imagination you are pure and real yo

Miracles are everywhere

shine
bright

celebrate life

THE
GOOD
LIFE

enjoy it

ve who you are   I see you   you make a difference to me   its okay to s
are doing a great job   it's okay to rest   you are learning so much
ave so much to be proud of and about   you are magnificent   there are
have what it takes   you are acing this   you are magnificent   you ar
do this   it's okay to ask for help   you worked hard for this   you are
can trust yourself   miracles are meant for you too   you are learning
e so much stronger than you think you are   this will teach you things
u can take the time you need   you get to decide   this is your life   yo
ll learn from this   you will be more experienced on the other side of
ny   you are fun   you are so full of life   you are the perfect one fo
nd what you are looking for   you will never regret going on this adv
meant to enjoy this time in your life   you can help others with your e
good   you are true   you are beautiful   you are smart   you are valu
will get through this   you will become the next version of yourself
to start over   you get to dream new dreams   you get to make this wha
get to reinvent yourself   you get to let go of what no longer serves
e worth protecting   you get to change   you get to grow   you get to evo
re phenomenal   you are going to figure this out   your life is worth
a gift   you are worth the time   you are a genius   you are gorgeous
e my favorite   you are the best you there ever was   you are something
on your own path   you are on your own journey   you are getting thro
matter in this world   you are fun to be with   you are enough in eve
re the real deal   you are interesting   you are doing a really good jo
the one   you are trustworthy   you are always a big surprise   you a
re one of a kind   you are just as important as everyone else   you get
u are safe   you are courageous   you made it through   you did it   yo
to do what you want to do now   you get to take the next step   you get
are kind   you are a rare bird   you are a beautiful soul   you are sma
u are part of this world   you belong   you are fun to be with   you a
e a talented human   you are on your way   you are brave enough to do
re magical   you have a beautiful heart   you are a warrior   you are w
u have the best ideas   you worked hard for this   you deserve every go
he strength to make it   you can climb that mountain   you can make it
re a miracle   you are a masterpiece   you are full of surprises   you a
e style   you are unique   you are creative   you can make it your own
can do this your own way   you can make this your own   you can put y
are good hearted   you are dependable   you are full of strength   yo
e made of love   you have the best laugh   you are thoughful   you are
someone I admire   you are someone to learn from   you are a gift to th
e the one I want to be with   you are the one I think about all the tim
are awesome   you have a wild imagination   you are pure and real   yo

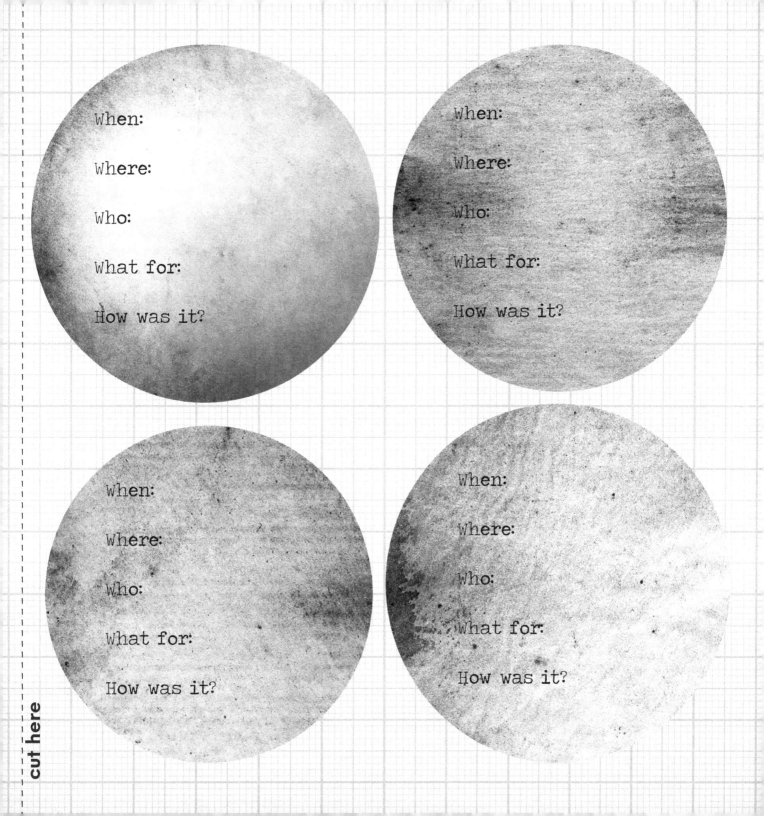

When:

Where:

Who:

What for:

How was it?

When:

Where:

Who:

What for:

How was it?

When:

Where:

Who:

What for:

How was it?

When:

Where:

Who:

What for:

How was it?

fe is maddening life is exhilirating life is wierd life is phenome
an adventure life is more than what it seems life is changing life
fe is good life is devastating life is chaotic life is precious 1
is stressful life is restorative life is colorful life is dull li
magical life is about love life is about learning life is connect
ife will break you life will grow you life will teach you life wil
hallenge you life will ask you life will be relentless life will l
l make you what you are meant to be life will let you experience cons
oing life will soften you life will toughen you up life will retur
e does not give up on you life will patiently wait for you to learn
s gorgeous life is in order life is a paradox life is a mystery
ife is lovely life holds gifts for you life wants you to notice lif
not always fair life can transform pain into wisdom life is here to
t to be lived life is meant to be experienced life is meant to be enj
fe will not leave you behind life is on your side life will let you
mined life is amazing life is surprising life is difficult life is
life is educating life is transformative life is perplexing life i
fe is maddening life is exhilirating life is wierd life is phenome
an adventure life is more than what it seems life is changing life
ife is good life is devastating life is chaotic life is precious 1
is stressful life is restorative life is colorful life is dull li
magical life is about love life is about learning life is connect
ife will break you life will grow you life will teach you life wil
hallenge you life will ask you life will be relentless life will l
l make you what you are meant to be life will let you experience cons
oing life will soften you life will toughen you up life will retur
e does not give up on you life will patiently wait for you to learn
s gorgeous life is in order life is a paradox life is a mystery
ife is lovely life holds gifts for you life wants you to notice lif
not always fair life can transform pain into wisdom life is here to
t to be lived life is meant to be experienced life is meant to be enj
will not leave you behind life is on your side life will let you le
mined life is amazing life is surprising life is difficult life is
life is educating life is transformative life is perplexing life i
fe is maddening life is exhilirating life is wierd life is phenome
an adventure life is more than what it seems life is changing life
ife is good life is devastating life is chaotic life is precious 1
is stressful life is restorative life is colorful life is dull li
magical life is about love life is about learning life is connect
ife will break you life will grow you life will teach you life wil
hallenge you life will ask you life will be relentless life will 1

All of life is a lesson

What are my most important relationships right now?

How do I feel about the state of the world right now?

What do I do in a typical day at this time in my life?

Am I taking good care of myself right now? Discuss ...

Am I feeling like my life is on track right now? Discuss ...

Do I have dreams and goals that I am working toward right now?

How am I feeling about getting older? Is it like I thought it would be?

What am I believing about the future right now?

Are there things that are bothering me each day consistently?

Do I trust myself? Do I make time to get really quiet and listen inside?

Do I treat myself with respect? Do I focus on self-respect?

What is something that almost always makes me laugh?

What is something that almost always refuels me with good energy?

When do I find myself feeling really good and happy and at peace?

Who always seems to leave me better than they found me?

What is a secret dream that I never really stop dreaming about?

What would be the perfect way for me to spend most of my time?

Who would I love to have as a life coach to help me every day?

Where is the place that I feel most like myself?

m on my own path   I am recovering   I am getting stronger   I am phen
good at lots of things   I am okay that I am not good at everything   I
am full of awe   I am ready for adventure   I am on a mission I am a m
letting go   I am holding on tight   I am figuring it out   I am often c
m a soul   I am a human being   I am an individual   I am part of it al
am letting myself begin again I am remembering the good things I have
I am a warrior   I am a gentle heart   I am brave   I am ready for a cha
m here to experience life   I am here to love others I am here to be lo
m gutsy   I am afraid of lots of things   I am curious   I am an artist
am a lover of music I am a lover of dancing   I am a lover of people
breathing   I am thinking   I am wondering   I am feeling I am talkin
m reinventing   I am building I am creating   I am dreaming   I am pla
art of creation I am looking for awe   I am noticing beauty I am a na
m starting over I am celebrating   I am grieving I am cleaning up a bi
am loved I am misunderstood I am seen   I am heard   I am not done livin
ull of life I am going through hard things right now   I am having a
n lucky I am blessed I am learning to accept this time in my life I a
a free spirit   I am unlearning   I am remembering   I am revisiting I am
in love with the earth   I am a lover of color   I am a happy person I
nding up for what I believe in I am standing up for others   I am doin
courageous I am working on my life I am focusing on self-respect I a
m powerful   I am strong   I am learning   I am beautiful in my own wa
I am alive   I am a part of the human family   I am beloved   I am a m
am on my own path   I am recovering   I am getting stronger   I am phen
good at lots of things   I am okay that I am not good at everything   I
am full of awe   I am ready for adventure   I am on a mission I am a m
letting go   I am holding on tight   I am figuring it out   I am often c
m a soul   I am a human being   I am an individual   I am part of it al
am letting myself begin again I am remembering the good things I have
I am a warrior   I am a gentle heart   I am brave   I am ready for a cha
m here to experience life   I am here to love others I am here to be lo
m gutsy   I am afraid of lots of things   I am curious   I am an artist
am a lover of music I am a lover of dancing   I am a lover of people
breathing   I am thinking   I am wondering   I am feeling I am talkin
m reinventing   I am building I am creating   I am dreaming   I am pla
art of creation I am looking for awe   I am noticing beauty I am a na
m starting over I am celebrating   I am grieving I am cleaning up a bi
am loved I am misunderstood I am seen   I am heard   I am not done livin
ull of life I am going through hard things right now   I am having a
n lucky I am blessed I am learning to accept this time in my life I a
a free spirit   I am unlearning   I am remembering   I am revisiting I am

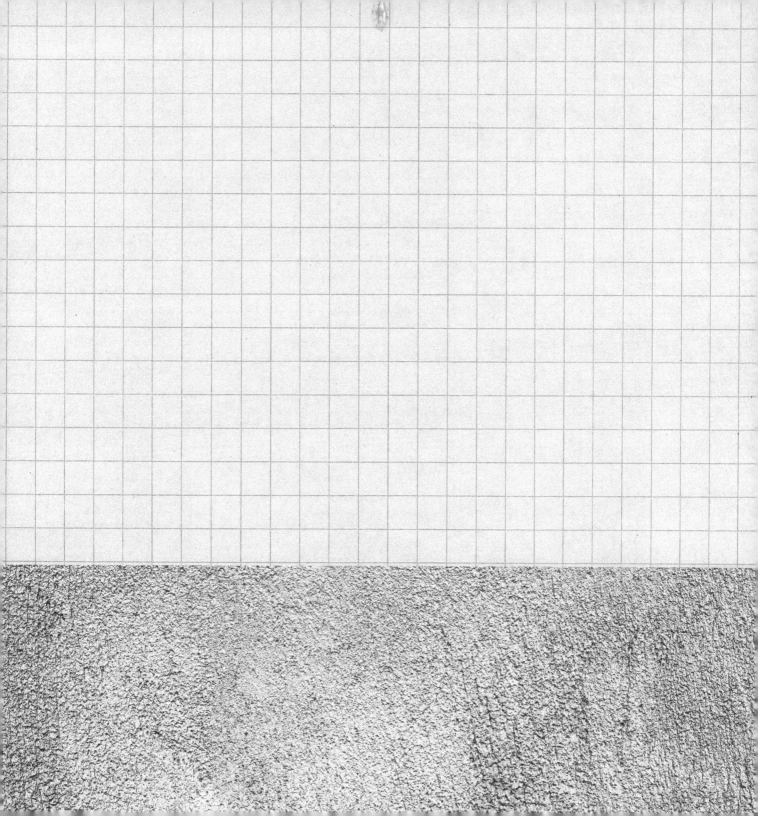

Move when it's time to move & be still when it's time to be still

I LIKE

I LOVE

I NEED

I KNOW

I EXPECT

I ADORE

I STRUGGLE WITH

I ROCK AT

I SECRETLY ADMIRE

I BELIEVE IN

I DO NOT ENJOY

I WANT

ve who you are   I see you   you make a difference to me   its okay to s
are doing a great job   it's okay to rest   you are learning so much
ave so much to be proud of and about   you are magnificent   there are
have what it takes   you are acing this   you are magnificent   you ar
do this   it's okay to ask for help   you worked hard for this   you are
can trust yourself   miracles are meant for you too   you are learning
e so much stronger than you think you are   this will teach you things
u can take the time you need   you get to decide   this is your life   yo
ll learn from this   you will be more experienced on the other side of
ny   you are fun   you are so full of life   you are the perfect one fo
ind what you are looking for   you will never regret going on this adv
meant to enjoy this time in your life   you can help others with your e
good   you are true   you are beautiful   you are smart   you are valu
u will get through this   you will become the next version of yourself
to start over   you get to dream new dreams   you get to make this wha
u get to reinvent yourself   you get to let go of what no longer serves
e worth protecting   you get to change   you get to grow   you get to evo
re phenomenal   you are going to figure this out   your life is worth
a gift   you are worth the time   you are a genius   you are gorgeous
e my favorite   you are the best you there ever was   you are something
on your own path   you are on your own journey   you are getting thro
u matter in this world   you are fun to be with   you are enough in eve
re the real deal   you are interesting   you are doing a really good jo
the one   you are trustworthy   you are always a big surprise   you a
re one of a kind   you are just as important as everyone else   you get
u are safe   you are courageous   you made it through   you did it   yo
to do what you want to do now   you get to take the next step   you get
are kind   you are a rare bird   you are a beautiful soul   you are sma
u are part of this world   you belong   you are fun to be with   you a
e a talented human   you are on your way   you are brave enough to do
re magical   you have a beautiful heart   you are a warrior   you are w
u have the best ideas   you worked hard for this   you deserve every go
he strength to make it   you can climb that mountain   you can make it
re a miracle   you are a masterpiece   you are full of surprises   you a
e style   you are unique   you are creative   you can make it your own
can do this your own way   you can make this your own   you can put y
u are good hearted   you are dependable   you are full of strength   yo
e made of love   you have the best laugh   you are thoughful   you are
someone I admire   you are someone to learn from   you are a gift to th
e the one I want to be with   you are the one I think about all the tim
are awesome   you have a wild imagination   you are pure and real   yo

Life is a challenge sometimes

I am thinking . . .

I think . . .

I am wondering . . .

I wonder . . .

I am feeling . . .

I feel . . .

cut here

fe is maddening   life is exhilirating   life is wierd   life is phenome
an adventure   life is more than what it seems   life is changing   lif
fe is good   life is devastating   life is chaotic   life is precious   l
is stressful   life is restorative   life is colorful   life is dull   li
magical   life is about love   life is about learning   life is connect
ife will break you   life will grow you   life will teach you   life wil
hallenge you   life will ask you   life will be relentless   life will l
l make you what you are meant to be   life will let you experience cons
oing   life will soften you   life will toughen you up   life will retur
e does not give up on you   life will patiently wait for you to learn
s gorgeous   life is in order   life is a paradox   life is a mystery
ife is lovely   life holds gifts for you   life wants you to notice   lif
ot always fair   life can transform pain into wisdom   life is here to
t to be lived   life is meant to be experienced   life is meant to be enj
fe will not leave you behind   life is on your side   life will let you
mined   life is amazing   life is surprising   life is difficult   life is
life is educating   life is transformative   life is perplexing   life i
fe is maddening   life is exhilirating   life is wierd   life is phenome
an adventure   life is more than what it seems   life is changing   lif
ife is good   life is devastating   life is chaotic   life is precious   l
is stressful   life is restorative   life is colorful   life is dull   li
magical   life is about love   life is about learning   life is connect
ife will break you   life will grow you   life will teach you   life wil
hallenge you   life will ask you   life will be relentless   life will l
l make you what you are meant to be   life will let you experience cons
oing   life will soften you   life will toughen you up   life will retur
e does not give up on you   life will patiently wait for you to learn
s gorgeous   life is in order   life is a paradox   life is a mystery
ife is lovely   life holds gifts for you   life wants you to notice   lif
ot always fair   life can transform pain into wisdom   life is here to
t to be lived   life is meant to be experienced   life is meant to be enj
will not leave you behind   life is on your side   life will let you le
mined   life is amazing   life is surprising   life is difficult   life is
life is educating   life is transformative   life is perplexing   life i
fe is maddening   life is exhilirating   life is wierd   life is phenome
an adventure   life is more than what it seems   life is changing   lif
ife is good   life is devastating   life is chaotic   life is precious   l
is stressful   life is restorative   life is colorful   life is dull   li
magical   life is about love   life is about learning   life is connect
ife will break you   life will grow you   life will teach you   life wil
hallenge you   life will ask you   life will be relentless   life will l

fun	awe	beauty	brave
travel	weird	whoa	funny
wow	lovely	learn	listen
cry	good	music	food
yum	this	here	now
us	me	you	mine
see	hear	taste	feel

m on my own path I am recovering I am getting stronger I am phen
 good at lots of things I am okay that I am not good at everything I
am full of awe I am ready for adventure I am on a mission I am a m
 letting go I am holding on tight I am figuring it out I am often c
m a soul I am a human being I am an individual I am part of it al
am letting myself begin again I am remembering the good things I have
 I am a warrior I am a gentle heart I am brave I am ready for a cha
m here to experience life I am here to love others I am here to be lo
m gutsy I am afraid of lots of things I am curious I am an artist
am a lover of music I am a lover of dancing I am a lover of people I
 breathing I am thinking I am wondering I am feeling I am talkir
m reinventing I am building I am creating I am dreaming I am pla
art of creation I am looking for awe I am noticing beauty I am a na
m starting over I am celebrating I am grieving I am cleaning up a bi
am loved I am misunderstood I am seen I am heard I am not done livir
ull of life I am going through hard things right now I am having a
n lucky I am blessed I am learning to accept this time in my life I a
a free spirit I am unlearning I am remembering I am revisiting I am
 in love with the earth I am a lover of color I am a happy person I
ding up for what I believe in I am standing up for others I am doin
courageous I am working on my life I am focusing on self-respect I a
m powerful I am strong I am learning I am beautiful in my own wa
 I am alive I am a part of the human family I am beloved I am a m
m on my own path I am recovering I am getting stronger I am phen
 good at lots of things I am okay that I am not good at everything I
am full of awe I am ready for adventure I am on a mission I am a m
 letting go I am holding on tight I am figuring it out I am often c
m a soul I am a human being I am an individual I am part of it al
am letting myself begin again I am remembering the good things I have
 I am a warrior I am a gentle heart I am brave I am ready for a cha
m here to experience life I am here to love others I am here to be lo
m gutsy I am afraid of lots of things I am curious I am an artist
am a lover of music I am a lover of dancing I am a lover of people I
 breathing I am thinking I am wondering I am feeling I am talkir
m reinventing I am building I am creating I am dreaming I am pla
art of creation I am looking for awe I am noticing beauty I am a na
m starting over I am celebrating I am grieving I am cleaning up a bi
am loved I am misunderstood I am seen I am heard I am not done livir
ull of life I am going through hard things right now I am having a
n lucky I am blessed I am learning to accept this time in my life I a
a free spirit I am unlearning I am remembering I am revisiting I am

Life is
a
beautiful
journey.